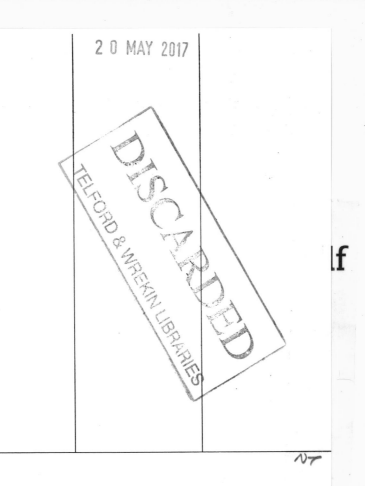

First published in 2011 in Great Britain by
Barrington Stoke Ltd
18 Walker St, Edinburgh, EH3 7LP

www.barringtonstoke.co.uk

Copyright © 2011 John Townsend
Illustrations © Daniel Atanasov

ISBN: 978-1-84299-776-5

Printed in China by Leo

# Contents

# Luc Pascal's Story

## France – 1767

We're scared.

My children are crying but no one must hear them. I can't let them make a sound. Not a whisper.

How can I tell a two-year-old someone wants to kill him? How can I tell a baby that no one must hear him?

We're hiding here in the darkness. Hiding under straw in a barn. We're praying the mob will pass by. Praying they won't find us. They have sticks and rocks and dogs ... and fire.

If they find us, we won't stand a chance.

Many years ago in this part of France, hundreds of men, women and children were hunted down and killed. Angry mobs – just like the one that's after us – got them and killed them. They burned them at the stake. The mob said they were werewolves.

All that was in the past. Things should be different now. I thought we'd be safe, hidden away in the forest out of harm's way. We were until the Beast came. Now the world has gone mad again and they all want blood. Ours.

There's almost no light. Only the moon. My fingers are trembling. It's hard to write.

But I must tell my story so someone knows the truth – the horror of our times. The horror of being a werewolf.

I need to tell the truth as I know it.

# Chapter 1
# Hidden Fear

For hundreds of years people have been scared of wolves.

Howls in the dead of night sent a chill through any forest. Wolf tracks in the snow terrified even the bravest hunter. Travellers had to watch out for hungry wolf packs waiting for them in the moonlight.

People told terrible stories as they sat around their camp fires. The wolves were never far away, prowling the icy hills. Danger was out there. Waiting. For hundreds of years wolves have been in our horror stories.

There were other tales too. Tales about wolves that ate human flesh. Such beasts, people said, looked like humans and had strange powers. What if a wolf could grow to twice its size and walk on two legs? Many people believed that wolf-men roamed the forests. Anyone they bit would become a werewolf, too.

So everyone was terrified of werewolves. People believed anyone might be one. If you were thought to be a werewolf, the mob would come for you. They took you away and burnt you alive.

For over a hundred years families were killed because of other people's fear and crazy beliefs. There were thousands and thousands of helpless victims. But at last the panic died down.

Then, in the 1760s, a new wolf terror swept through France. A large beast began killing children. Many people thought an evil werewolf was on the prowl. But it wasn't just the Beast that scared everyone. Mad panic began again.

The French called the animal La Bête (the Beast). For almost three years, everyone in the hills in the middle of France lived in fear. No one knew when the wolf-beast would strike next. And when it did, terror spread like a forest fire.

When the Beast killed, mobs went out to hunt for werewolves in the forest. They had flame-torches and knives and they were ready to kill anyone they thought might be a werewolf.

No one was safe. No one at all.

# Chapter 2
# The First Attack

The eyes were watching. They stared out from the deepest shadows. Narrow eyes, dark orange with evil black centres. Each with a speck of icy silver. Mean eyes and hungry, always on the look-out. Waiting. For prey.

The sheep were restless. They sensed something was there – somewhere in the darkness of the forest. But sheep didn't need to be scared. Other prey was on the hillside now.

The girl walked across the fields in the dying light. A red sun was dipping behind the woods and long shadows stretched over the grass. She shook the bucket in her arms and the lambs ran to her. She opened the gate to the sheep pen.

The eyes watched everything the girl did. She didn't hear the snarl and cracking of twigs as the Beast crept out of the shadows.

The girl's father was worried. It was late and his daughter was still out there in the darkness. It never took her this long to feed the lambs. So he set out across the field with his lantern. As he called across the hillside, the eyes blinked. They watched him enter the sheep pen. They saw him lift his lantern high and cry out. The father dropped to his knees beside the girl's torn body. Beside her in the mud were foot-prints. Prints from a huge beast with claws.

That was the first attack. It was in the summer of 1764. A few nights later, two more children went missing. They, too, were found at the edge of the forest with their throats torn open and their bodies half-eaten.

No child was safe. For miles around, all children had to stay indoors. No one was let out to play. A killer beast was out there. Waiting. Snarling. Watching ...

# Chapter 3
## Growing Terror

People began to tell stories about the wolf-beast.

Just after the first children were killed, a woman told of her narrow escape. She was out in her field when a large beast rushed from the trees towards her. She said it swept past her cows and leapt straight at her. One of her bulls had big horns and charged at the Beast and it ran off. The woman said the animal was as big as a donkey with thick dark hair all over its body. No one believed her. But as winter came, with ever darker nights, the fear grew.

When Christmas came, no one dared to go out singing carols. No one dared to open a door to strangers. On snowy nights everyone stayed indoors. Some mornings, the snow was stained red. Bloody tracks led into the woods – the tracks of a large wolf-beast. Another child would be missing.

A farmer went out in a snow-storm to look for his missing son. He found him. The boy was lying in the sheep shed. He was dead, with bites all over his body. His father carried him home, laid him on the floor of the kitchen and put a blanket over him. A noise outside made the farmer turn and look up. A hairy face was staring in at him through the window, with eyes like fire. The man grabbed a gun and fired but the snarling face ducked. The farmer ran outside to face the Beast, which howled and then headed off across an orchard. It looked like a man in an animal skin. Its footprints in the snow were huge and showed it could make giant leaps.

People said the animal must be far more than just a wolf.

A woman was walking through the frosty fields and saw the same strange beast. She said it stood like a man but was covered with hair from head to foot. It had short ears, a long tail and a nose like a pig's snout. When the Beast saw her, it rushed towards her so she ran for her life. When she got to the village, she looked behind her but the animal had gone.

A year after the first attack, after many children had been killed or gone missing, a farmer came face to face with the Beast. Late one summer night he was cutting corn in his field in the light of the moon. He looked up to see something moving through the corn. He heard a growl but the animal was hidden by tall stalks.

At first the farmer thought one of his farm dogs was running to him. But suddenly a snarling beast leapt at his neck. He felt its hot breath on his face as spit flew from its fangs. It had a vile smell. Its eyes glowed red, flashing in the moonlight.

The farmer grabbed a pitch-fork. He stabbed at the snarling teeth and fought off the animal. It ran back into the forest and the man limped home. He couldn't speak for hours. He was frozen with terror. When at last he was able to talk, he said he'd been attacked by something like a wolf that reared up on its back legs. It had a wide hairy chest and a long tail with fur on the end, like a lion's. Whatever it was, the farmer was sure it was after him and that it was a man-eater.

Local people set out for revenge. They had to stop the Beast. But some of the hunters warned it might be a werewolf. They'd have to be careful. Bites from its fangs would turn everyone into werewolves! Then what would happen?

Everyone was frightened. No one knew what might happen next. But worse was to come.

# Chapter 4
# Growing Danger

Danger was never far away. It was always risky to be out alone, so people thought they'd be safe with others around. But that wasn't so. One evening the wild beast attacked a group of 11-year-olds near the village of Villeret.

Five boys and two girls were looking after cows on a mountain. They all had sticks with sharp blades tied on the ends – just in case something attacked them.

Suddenly the Beast ran at them and clamped its jaws on one boy's head. His friends stabbed at the animal and it let go, but then it grabbed another boy by the arm. It dragged him into a marsh. Jacques, the biggest boy, lifted his spear and chased it. The other children ran after it too. They caught up with the Beast as it tried to wade through thick mud. Jacques waded in after it and jabbed it with his stick. They all screamed and threw their sticks at it. A man nearby heard them and came running. He yelled and the Beast ran off. It left its victim with a badly bitten arm.

Jacques and his friends were heroes. Even King Louis XV heard about how brave they had been and sent them money as a reward.

That same year, there was another famous fight with La Bête. Once more the King paid a reward. This time the Beast tried to eat a mother and her children. Madame

Jouve was only a small woman but she fought the Beast to save her three children from its jaws. Its fangs ripped into her then clamped onto her son's head. Madame Jouve fought back. She had no weapons but she threw rocks at the Beast. She was badly hurt and one of her sons was killed. The local mayor wrote – "The skin of his skull was falling off, his cheek was ripped and his nose was torn away to the root. He died within three days."

The Beast attacked mainly women and children. That was because they were the ones who were often up in the hills on their own, looking after the sheep. They were easy prey. The men did the heavy work in the lower fields. They worked in groups and were armed with spades or forks.

The Beast knew who were easiest to kill. Some people said that was because it was part man. A werewolf. They thought the Beast could change from man to wolf and back again.

That made sense of another story people were telling. Three women were on their way to church one evening. Just as they got to the woods, a stranger came out of the shadows. He said he'd walk with them through the trees to help them find their way. The women had a bad feeling about this stranger. They said they wanted to walk on their own. Then the man touched one of the women on her arm. She looked down in horror and saw his hand was hairy and like a claw. The women ran off and met some soldiers. The soldiers told the terrified women that the Beast had just been seen in the woods. They told them to go home and lock their doors.

Another story told of two women who met a man on their way to church. As the man spoke to them, the wind blew his shirt open and they saw that his body was covered with thick hair. They screamed and ran. Later, someone at the church told them that he'd seen the Beast on the very same path.

Once more there was panic in all the nearby villages. Who were the werewolves? Were they beasts sent by the devil to stop people going to church? Many people were too scared to go out. They didn't even go to work. If this went on much longer, everyone would starve. No one was looking after the fields or the cattle. The curse of the werewolf was starting to harm everyone. It was time to fight back.

Farmers set traps but they caught nothing. Some hunters even dressed as women and stood alone on the hills. They hoped to act as bait while gun-men lay in wait. But nothing worked. The Beast was still free. Howls still chilled the moonlit forest – as well as the awful screams from the next victim.

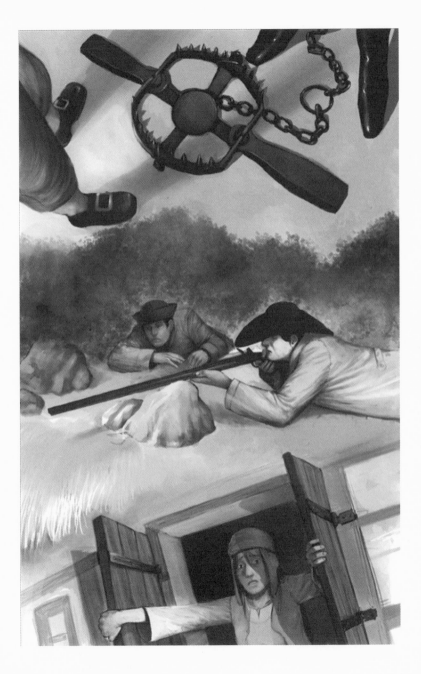

# Chapter 5
# Fighting Back

Something had to be done. People from miles around held a meeting. They knew they couldn't get rid of the Beast on their own. They needed an army with guns. So they wrote to the King for help.

King Louis XV sent a troop of soldiers to kill the Beast. At first the soldiers were cross. Why should they sort out the troubles of simple farmers? They didn't believe in werewolves. It must just be a big wolf. So why couldn't a hunter with a few dogs sort it out? The King's soldiers were far too important to bother with an animal. Their job was to fight wars and protect the King. But then they saw the Beast for themselves.

The soldiers were amazed to see such a large animal. They weren't sure if it was a wolf, a bear or a lion. Whatever it was, they shot at it. When the Beast fell, no one wanted to get close to check if it was dead. One soldier crept up to take a closer look – but not too close. He could see that it was big and hairy, like nothing he'd seen before. He reported back that they'd killed the Beast. The soldiers told the King their job was done. But they should have taken a closer look at the body. By nightfall it had gone.

Before long the killings started again. More children vanished. The Beast was still out there. People were even more scared now. They began to move away to other parts of

France. Farms were left empty. Villages were deserted. The people who stayed sent another letter to the King. This time his troops were too busy to help. Instead, the King sent François Antoine. He was a full-time expert wolf-hunter with a pack of blood-hounds.

Towards the end of 1765, Antoine, his dogs and a team of gunmen tracked down a large animal in the forest. They closed in. They drove the Beast to a cave they thought must be its den. They set up a long net to catch it, just as something moved in the shadows. The dogs barked and sprang. A huge creature darted out through the trees to the edge of the wood. It dived through a hole in the net. Antoine lifted his gun and fired.

The Beast fell and the gunmen sounded their horns. They'd got him! Suddenly the animal moved again. It leapt to its feet. A gunman fired a second time. The shot hit its body but the animal staggered on through

the smoke. In the deathly silence that followed, the creature gasped and fell in the mud. It rolled over with a final growl and lay still. Dead at last!

The hunters took a close look at the dead body. Antoine and his men had killed a very large grey wolf. He later wrote: "We never saw such a big wolf as this one. This must be the fearsome beast that caused so much damage."

There were many scars on the wolf's body. They must have come from all its fights with people with sticks. But now, at last, the wolf lay dead. Its body was taken away, stuffed and sent to the King. Antoine became a hero. People gave him money and awards. They cheered him and held parties to celebrate.

With Christmas coming, people went back into the forest to gather wood and holly.

They didn't think they were being watched any more. But they were.

On the 21st December, a little girl's remains were found in the woods. There was hardly anything left of her. Nine-year-old Agnès Mourges was missing. She was never seen again. The worst was feared. The Beast must still be out there. As winter turned to spring, there were 14 savage attacks on children nearby. The dreaded beast wasn't dead after all – but alive ... and hungry.

The King gave orders for the biggest hunt ever in France to begin. Hundreds of hunters on the best horses and with the best dogs swept through the countryside. They killed hundreds of wolves. Any animal that moved in the forest was likely to be shot. But one kept hidden. It waited in the darkness of its cave. The eyes kept watching. Waiting. Always ready for the next attack.

# Chapter 6
# A New Hero

Stories and rumours spread like wild fire. Many people believed the wolf that Antoine killed had come back to life. They believed werewolves could never be killed. The word went round that the Beast must have been a messenger from Hell after all.

The next winter was calmer. Only a few children went missing. Some people said the evil beast was getting scared because everyone was now going to church more often. What they didn't understand was that fewer children went on the hills in bad weather. The Beast must have gone back to eating sheep and cows – until the spring.

As spring came the attacks on people began again. No one really knew how many children were killed when the evenings grew lighter. Many families were too scared to admit their children were missing. Some believed the werewolf only attacked wicked people, so parents said nothing if a child didn't come home from the hills.

Then another hunter arrived. Jean Chastel was a local farmer and inn-keeper who said he'd been sent by God to kill the Beast. He set about getting an army of local people to go through the forest beating their sticks. On 19th June 1767, about 300 people with dogs and sticks crashed through the forest. They hoped to flush out the Beast once and for all. Jean Chastel's mind was made up. He was

going to shoot the Beast as it fled from the forest. And he wouldn't miss.

The story of what happened next is now told all over France. Jean Chastel said he stood alone in a gully just outside the forest. He felt sure the Beast would have to run right past him to escape. He opened his prayer book and began to pray as he waited for the Beast. Sure enough, there was a whispering of leaves behind him in the forest.

Eyes glared at him from the shadows. Narrow eyes, dark orange with evil black centres. Each with a speck of icy silver. Savage eyes that flashed with rage. The Beast crept into the open with an angry growl.

Jean Chastel finished his prayer and slowly closed the book. He turned, looked up and saw the Beast coming nearer. He took off his glasses, put them in his pocket and slowly loaded his rifle with two silver bullets. As the

Beast leapt at him, he raised his gun and fired twice.

The crack of the rifle shots ripped through the forest. A bullet pierced the Beast's heart. It fell with a roar and died in an instant. As the smoke cleared, Jean Chastel put down his gun and said softly, "Good. You will kill no more."

It is said that at the spot where the Beast died, the grass no longer grows.

No one really knows what happened next. Some reports say the Beast's body was opened up, that Jean Chastel found a child's collar bone inside its belly. The streets were crowded when farmers carried a dead wolf through the town to show the Beast was dead at last. But a legend says the real body of the Beast had to be hidden. It was too terrible for people to see. It looked too much like a human.

No one knows what happened to the Beast's remains. One report says La Bête was burned. Another says the body was buried when it began to rot – it had been on display too long. Another story says that when the body was being taken to the King, it vanished somewhere on the way. No one knows how or where.

All the mystery led to yet another belief that the werewolf was still alive. Some people thought that Jean Chastel was not a hero at all, but that he was a secret friend of the Beast. Had he trained it to attack? No one had ever seen Jean Chastel and the Beast at the same time. Many people said the two of them were really the same thing. Jean Chastel, they said, must be a werewolf.

# Chapter 7

## The Curse Returns

## Luc Pascal's Story

Now it's back to my story and to why I'm hiding in this barn in the forest. I'm hiding my family from the mob out there. It's a matter of life and death.

And now you know why we're so scared. The Beast may be dead, but fear is alive. Our worries are far from over, after all.

It's Christmas 1767. Jean Chastel killed the Beast last summer. We should be at peace again, but it seems the dead of winter brings out more crazy beliefs and fear. The mob believes the 'messenger from hell' is still alive – in this forest. They want revenge. And when better than tonight in the snow under a full moon?

The hounds have already smelled us out. I can hear them howling and barking as I write these shaky words. They're after our blood and there's nothing I can do.

I've always had to stay hidden. It's the price I have to pay for the way I look.

It was the same for my father and brother. And now my son has the same curse. We were all born with dark patches on our skin. Our faces and backs have hair growing all over. However much I shave, the hair grows back. I used to think I really did have the face of a wolf. But I now know it's a skin problem that runs in our family. We can do nothing about it.

People say I must have got my hairy body from falling asleep under a full moon. They say sleeping in the moon-light turns you into a werewolf. Others say I've drunk water from a wolf's foot-print. That's supposed to turn you into a werewolf, too. But it's all nonsense.

One poor family was burned in their beds the other night. Their cottage was razed to the ground. All because they were ill. They'd eaten bread that was mouldy and rotten. That's all the poor have to eat sometimes. But it causes a terrible illness called Saint Anthony's Fire. It makes people grunt, shake and look wild – just like a wolf. The mob called them werewolves from the devil. So they set fire to their home.

Last week a boy in the village was dragged into the forest and a crowd of angry people stoned him to death. He was ill, too. He'd been bitten by a wolf with rabies. The disease took hold of his body. He began to froth at the mouth and growl from the fever. They all said he was turning into a werewolf. He didn't stand a chance.

When people see me they either laugh or turn away in fear. Or sometimes they throw stones. Some hate me for the way I look. They shout cruel things. They say I must be from the devil and must be destroyed. That's why I try to stay out of sight. But someone saw me when I was out gathering wood this morning. They called me the son of the Beast. So now the mob is after my blood. And they're just outside.

My wife and children are asleep at last. I've covered them with straw. The only way they'll be saved is if I give myself up. I must write these last words before I go out to face the hounds. They'll rip me apart but it's the only way to save the others. I hope it's over quickly.

I hope my story will tell the world of these terrible times and of the danger of foolish beliefs. As long as we live in darkness and fear, there will be cruel people who do terrible things. They believe that only they have the truth and the right to use force on others. They hate anyone who is different.

I can only hope that one day people will know better.

A howl just came from the hills. Then all fell silent. A real wolf. It has saved my life!

As soon as the mob heard it, they turned to head for the hills. The dogs and flaming torches are moving away through the forest. All is quiet here again.

We're spared – just in time. They're after the wolf now and nothing will stop them.

I can't believe our luck. I've escaped the werewolf's curse. The danger has passed.

At least, for now.

# Chapter 8
# Check the Facts

The story of La Bête has become a legend with all kinds of doubts now. It's hard to believe all of it. Did some of the things in this book really happen?

These are some of the key facts behind the story ...

There are many records that show a real beast killed about 100 people in France in the 1760s. All the accounts are different. They all have different stories about the attacks and about how many people were killed. Church records give the names and dates of the Beast's victims.

One account says there were 210 attacks, 113 deaths and 49 injuries. Ninety-eight of the dead victims were partly eaten.

At least five times, large wolves were killed. Each time people thought they'd got La Bête. But each time the attacks went on after the killing. The last beast was killed in June 1767. The attacks stopped after that.

Never at any other point in history has just one beast killed so many humans or taken so long to be caught. Many people saw the Beast in daylight and reported it. Most historians are sure it really existed.

The terrified farmers and villagers of central France were sure that there was a werewolf in their forests. They feared the

werewolf trials of 1520 to 1630 might return –
when over 30,000 people were accused of
being werewolves and sent to their deaths.

The writer Robert Louis Stevenson
(1850–94) wrote – "If all the wolves had been
as this wolf, they would have changed the
history of man."

At the time of the attacks, a Paris
newspaper wrote that La Bête was bigger
than a wolf, had red fur and a black back.
The paper also suggested that the Beast was
a cross-breed of a wolf and a hyena.

Forty years after this story, there were
more attacks in the south-east of France. At
least 21 children were killed by another
mystery beast.

Some experts think La Bête may have
been a Dire Wolf. These animals were larger
and more powerful than today's grey wolf.
They killed by crushing victims to death in

their jaws. Most people think they died out about 10,000 years ago. But did a few survive?

People all around the world have believed in werewolves down the ages. Some say that 'wolf people' changed into wolves at night, when the moon was full. In wolf form, werewolves attack people to eat them. Then they change back to a human by daylight.

'Wer' is an Old English word for man so a 'werewolf' is half man, half-wolf.

Sometimes people with a mental illness have believed they're werewolves. The special word for this sickness is called 'lycanthropy'.

Some people who were thought to be werewolves had diseases or medical conditions.

Human werewolf syndrome (also called hypertrichosis = 'extra hair'): Hair grows all over the body or on parts that are normally hair-free, such as the face or hands. Today people can be treated for this condition.

Rabies: This virus attacks the nervous system of animals and humans. You catch it by being bitten by an infected animal, such as a dog or wolf. If you have rabies, you foam at the mouth and seem to 'go mad' with fever. Today rabies is rare and can be treated – but not in the 1760s.

Saint Anthony's Fire: In 1151 many people living in the French village Pont Saint Esprit seemed to go mad. They ran crazily in the streets, their arms and legs felt as if they were on fire. Were they turning into werewolves? In fact they were ill with something called Saint Anthony's Fire. This horrible illness comes from eating bad mouldy bread made from rye flour.

Today there are statues of La Bête in parts of France where the Beast was said to live. Everyone in France knows the stories. Even today, the French have a saying – "When the twigs crack, don't whistle." (Just in case the Beast returns).

Don't have nightmares!

Barrington Stoke would like to thank all its readers for commenting on the manuscript before publication and in particular:

Leon Bryson
Rowan Chalmers
Bryn Davis
Erin Dawson
Ryan King
Jake Markidis
Jack Ramsey
Florence Rogerson

### Zombie!
### by
### Tommy Donbavand

Nathan thought he knew all about zombies. They're dead. They like eating brains. But he didn't know they liked to party. Until he met Jake. Jake's been dead for 60 years but that doesn't stop him having a good time. This party's sure to be a SCREAM!

### Scrum!
### by
### Tom Palmer

Steven's mad for Rugby League. His dad even reckons he'll go pro one day. Then his mum drops a bombshell. They're moving down south with her new boyfriend. To the land of Rugby Union. When the Union team wants Steven and the League scouts come calling, he faces the hardest choice of his life ...

You can order these books directly from our website at
www.barringtonstoke.co.uk

More fab books from Barrington Stoke